WORKBOOK TO ACCOMPANY

Music

IN THEORY AND PRACTICE

VOLUME II

Ninth Edition

Bruce Benward
Late of the University of Wisconsin–Madison

Marilyn Saker
Eastern Michigan University

McGraw Hill Education

WORKBOOK TO ACCOMPANY MUSIC IN THEORY AND PRACTICE, VOLUME II, NINTH EDITION

Published by McGraw-Hill Education, 2 Penn Plaza, New York, NY 10121. Copyright © 2015 by McGraw-Hill Education. All rights reserved. Printed in the United States of America. No part of this publication may be reproduced or distributed in any form or by any means, or stored in a database or retrieval system, without the prior written consent of McGraw-Hill Education, including, but not limited to, in any network or other electronic storage or transmission, or broadcast for distance learning.

Some ancillaries, including electronic and print components, may not be available to customers outside the United States.

This book is printed on acid-free paper.

1 2 3 4 5 6 7 8 9 0 QVS/QVS 1 0 9 8 7 6 5 4

ISBN 978-0-07-749333-2
MHID 0-07-749333-8

Contents

Preface

The workbooks to accompany *Music in Theory and Practice,* volumes 1 and 2, provide assignments to augment, in depth and breadth, those printed in the texts. The chapters of the workbooks bear the same titles as those of the texts and are directly correlated with them. The compositions in the anthology sections are referred to in the assignments, but the instructor is free to use these pieces in any way he or she feels is appropriate.

The workbooks contain three different types of assignments:

1. *Drill.* This type of assignment acquaints students with the material in the corresponding chapters of the text. In general, the topics are isolated from surrounding musical context to permit a grasp of the more obvious and elementary aspects. Learning to spell chords in various keys, distinguishing between chords in isolation, and identifying musical designs in artificially prepared situations are examples of drill exercises.

2. *Analysis.* This type of assignment acquaints students with music literature, permits them to view chapter material in its actual setting, and allows them to observe conformity to as well as digression from the norm. These exercises will also improve sight-reading ability and dexterity in analysis.

3. *Composition.* After completing the extensive drill and comprehensive analysis assignments provided by these workbooks, students are encouraged to try their own hands at employing musical ideas, chord progressions, phrase relationships, and so on, in the context of a musical composition. This comprises the ultimate test of a student's comprehension. If the devices that were drilled and analyzed can be successfully manipulated in a composition, one of the most important goals in the study of music theory has been achieved.

The workbooks include guided review and self-testing sections. Each chapter contains a suggested strategy for reviewing and learning the material. Students often find that the study skills they have developed for other courses do not work well in learning music theory. The guided review sections present a step-by-step process involving reading, playing musical examples, and writing, which will help ensure success in learning the material.

Each chapter concludes with a sample chapter test covering the essential concepts of the chapter. Answers for all chapter tests are contained in a section beginning on page 227. These tests allow the student to identify areas of strength and weakness before, rather than during, examinations.

Resources available from the McGraw-Hill Online Learning Center for this workbook include assignment templates compatible with Finale® music notation software and recordings for a majority of the compositions included in the anthology (recordings are identified with the following graphic: ♫). For instructors, a printable version of the corresponding *Workbook Solutions Manual* is available in addition to supplemental drill and testing materials. Visit www.mhhe.com/mtp9 for these items.

CHAPTER 1
Late Renaissance Polyphony

A. Refer to Lassus's *Sicut rosa* from *Cantiones Duarum Vocum* on page 190. Provide a complete analysis of *Sicut rosa* using the analysis of *Beatus homo* in Chapter 1 of the textbook as a model.
  1. Indicate the intervals between the two voices throughout.
  2. Circle and label all dissonant intervals:
     a. Unaccented passing tone
     b. Accented passing tone
     c. Suspension
     d. Portamento
     e. Nota cambiata
  3. Indicate all imitation by marking with a dotted line, a highlighter, or in any other appropriate manner.
  4. Name also:
     a. The mode of the composition
     b. The accidentals and the reason for their use
     c. The cadence points and the types of cadences used
     d. The treatment of the text—whether syllabic or melismatic

Text	Translation
Sicut rosa,	Just as a rose,
sicut rosa inter spinas illas audit speciem,	Just as a rose among thorns lends its beauty even to them,
sic renustat suam Virgo Maria progeniem, Maria progeniem,	In the same way the Virgin Mary imparts her grace and charm over all her subjects,
germinavit enim florem,	From her has sprung a flower,
qui vitalem dat odorem, qui vitalem dat odorem.	Whose aroma is the gift of life.

B. Apply the same analytical techniques described in Section A of this chapter to Lassus's *Sancti mei* from *Cantiones Duarum Vocum* on page 187:
  1. Indicate the intervals between the two voices throughout.
  2. Circle and label all dissonant intervals.
  3. Indicate all imitation by marking with a dotted line, a highlighter, or in any other appropriate manner.
  4. Name also:
     a. The mode of the composition
     b. The accidentals and the reason for their use
     c. The cadence points and the types of cadences used
     d. The treatment of the text—whether syllabic or melismatic

Text	Translation
Sancti mei, sancti mei,	My divine people, my divine people
qui in isto saeculo certamen habuistis,	Who in this world have known only hard labor and conflict,
mercedem laborum vestrorum ego reddam vobis,	I shall give to you satisfaction for your endeavors,
ego reddam vobis, ego reddam vobis.	For your endeavors, for your endeavors.

C. The following short excerpt contains a number of stylistic errors—musical devices that were foreign to the strict sacred vocal style of the sixteenth century.

1. Find each error and place a number on the score at the point of the error.
2. In the blanks below the score, indicate the nature of the error.
3. The first error is recorded correctly in the example (Ex. 1).

Composition containing errors:

Errors:

(Ex.) 1. __A note should not be tied to a succeeding note of longer value._____

2. _____

3. _____

4. _____

5. _____

6. _____

7. _____

8. _____

9. _____

10. _____

11. _____

12. _____

D. Refer to the *Benedictus* from *Missa pro defunctis* by Lassus on page 186. Apply the same analytical techniques described in Section A to this composition in three parts.

1. Indicate the intervals between the three voices throughout. Remember to assess the intervals according to the lowest-sounding voice.

2. Circle and label all dissonant intervals:

    a. Unaccented passing tone

    b. Accented passing tone

    c. Suspension

    d. Portamento

    e. Nota cambiata

3. Indicate all imitation by marking with a dotted line, a highlighter, or in any other appropriate manner.

4. Name also:

    a. The mode of the composition

    b. The accidentals and the reason for their use

    c. The cadence points and the types of cadences used

    d. The treatment of the text—whether syllabic or melismatic

Review

1. Review the consonant and dissonant intervals on pages 5–6 of the textbook. Every dissonant interval should be circled in your analysis and explained as one of the dissonance types listed on pages 6–10.

2. Review the dissonance types on pages 6–10. Study the musical examples illustrating each device, and play them over to hear the musical effect of the dissonance (singing them with a friend is even better). Pay particular attention to the decorations of suspensions, which may confuse you when you see them in a work you are analyzing. The nota cambiata also deserves special consideration because it is unique to the sixteenth-century style.

3. Study the section on melody on page 10, paying particular attention to the treatment of skips in a melody. Stepwise motion in the opposite direction preceding and following a skip has the effect of "smoothing out" the skip and thus diminishing its impact on the flow of the melody. Note the intervals that are avoided: ascending M6ths, descending 6ths, 7ths, diminished and augmented intervals, and skips greater than an octave. What intervals are allowed as skips?

4. Examine the list of common note values and note values that do not occur on pages 10–12. The subject of rhythm in sixteenth-century counterpoint is very complex, and the summary presented here is far from exhaustive. Look at individual voices of one of the works cited in the textbook and observe the rhythmic material in relation to the summary in the textbook.

5. Find several examples of clausula vera in the works cited in the textbook. Can you find a clausula vera that is not preceded by a suspension?

6. Listen to examples of sixteenth-century music (Palestrina, Lassus, Victoria, and others) to gain a sense of the style. Careful listening and performing the music are necessary to gain an appreciation of the style.

Test Yourself 1

Answers are on page 225.

1. Analyze the excerpt from *Justus cor suum tradet* quoted below by labeling each interval between the voices.
2. Circle all dissonances and label each one. Use Figure 1.31 on page 17 of the textbook as a model for this chapter.
3. Label the beginning of each point of imitation by drawing a line between the first note of each line.
4. In measure 6, a B♭ appears in the lower voice. Why is this B♭ necessary?
5. Examine all the note values in each line. Do you observe any deviations from the principles stated on pages 10–12?
6. A clausula vera occurs in measure_____.
7. The mode of this composition is_____.

Lassus: *Justus cor suum tradet* from *Cantiones Duarum Vocum*, mm. 1–12.

CHAPTER 2
Two-Voice Eighteenth-Century Counterpoint

A. Have a harpsichord or piano major play Invention no. 1 in C Major by Bach (page 131). Arrange it for two instruments or sing it in class on a syllable such as *la, lu,* or *ta.*

   1. Do a Roman numeral analysis and/or macro analysis of this invention.

   2. Above and below the score indicate the following:

      a. Each statement of the motive and countermotive

      b. All segments of the sequences

      c. Free material

      d. Motive-derived or countermotive-derived material

      e. The various sections of the two-part invention

      f. The types of cadences that punctuate the composition

   3. Discuss in class:

      a. The similarities and differences between this invention and the one analyzed in Chapter 2 of the textbook (Invention no. 4 in D Minor)

      b. The handling of dissonance

B. Write a two-part invention in eighteenth-century-style counterpoint.

   1. Pattern the form of your invention after no. 1 of Bach's inventions (refer to page 131 in the anthology).

   2. Write the composition for any instrument or instruments that can be played in class.

   3. Make up a *motive* of your own or use one of the following.

   4. Perform the composition in class. Then, have the class sing each student's composition on a syllable such as *la, lu,* or *ta.*

C. Using the same approach as in Section A of this chapter, provide a complete analysis of Invention no. 13 in A Minor by Bach (page 132). Have a harpsichord or piano major play the invention. Then, sing it in class on a syllable such as *la, lu,* or *ta.*

1. Do a Roman numeral analysis and/or macro analysis of this invention.
2. Above and below the score indicate the following:
    a. Each statement of the motive and countermotive
    b. All segments of the sequences
    c. Free material
    d. Motive-derived or countermotive-derived material
    e. The various sections of the two-part invention
    f. The types of cadences that punctuate the composition
3. Discuss in class:
    a. The similarities and differences between this invention and the one analyzed in Chapter 2 of the textbook (Invention no. 4 in D Minor)
    b. The handling of dissonance

Review

1. Review the description of a typical two-part invention on pages 29–35 of the textbook. Pay particular attention to the musical examples and how the various motives and sequences are labeled. Study Figure 2.4 in detail.
2. Study the section on writing two-voice counterpoint on pages 36–40. Review in particular the section on avoiding parallel perfect intervals. The restrictions on parallel perfect intervals are more stringent in two-part writing than in four-part chorale styles.
3. Listen to a recording of the two-part inventions or play several at a keyboard. Careful listening is an important adjunct to study of the text.

Test Yourself 2

Answers are on page 226.

1. Examine the following two-part invention and listen to a recording or play it.

2. Measure 1 contains a statement of the _____.

3. The lower part in measure 2 is the _____ in imitation. The interval of imitation is a(n) _____.

    The right-hand part in measure 2 is the _____.

4. Measures 4–6 are a good example of a _____.

5. The second part of the invention begins in measure _____. It is in the _____ key (relation to the tonic).

6. In measure 27 in the right hand there is a statement of the _____ in the _____ key.

7. Provide a Roman numeral analysis of this invention. Refer to Figure 2.4 in the textbook as a model.

8. Invention number 10 is in _____ sections.

Bach: Invention no. 10 in G Major from *Fifteen Two-Part Inventions*, BWV 781.

CHAPTER 3
The Fugue

A. Refer to Bach's Fugue no. 6 in D Minor from *The Well-Tempered Clavier,* Book I, on page 125. Have a harpsichord or piano major play this three-voice fugue. Arrange it for three instruments or sing it in class on a syllable such as *la, lu,* or *ta.*
   1. Do a Roman numeral analysis and/or macro analysis of this fugue.
   2. Use a highlighter or any other appropriate way to indicate or label the following:
      a. Each statement of the subject, answer, and countersubject
      b. The type of answer—whether tonal or real
      c. All segments of sequences
      d. The larger sections of the composition: the exposition and all episodes and entries
      e. The various keys represented in the composition
      f. The cadence points and the types of cadences used
      g. Any bridges, codettas, or links

B. Using the same approach as in Section A of this chapter, provide a complete analysis of Bach's Fugue no. 7 in E-flat Major from *The Well-Tempered Clavier,* Book I, on page 128.
   1. Do a Roman numeral analysis and/or macro analysis of this fugue.
   2. Use a highlighter or any other appropriate way to indicate or label the following:
      a. Each statement of the subject, answer, and countersubject
      b. The type of answer—whether tonal or real
      c. All segments of sequences
      d. The larger sections of the composition: the exposition and all episodes and entries
      e. The various keys represented in the composition
      f. The cadence points and the types of cadences used
      g. Any bridges, codettas, or links
   3. Compare the form and general makeup of this fugue with that of the Fugue no. 6 in D Minor (Section A of this chapter).

C. Write the exposition of a three-voice fugue in eighteenth-century-style counterpoint.
   1. Pattern the form of the exposition after the Bach Fugue in C Minor in Chapter 3 of the textbook.
   2. Write the exposition for any instrument or instrumental combination that can assure a performance in class.
   3. Use one of the fugue subjects in the following list.
   4. Perform the compositions in class. Sing each student's composition on a syllable such as *la, lu,* or *ta.*

Subjects

1. Fischer: subject

Answers

1. Fischer: answer

Subjects

2. Fischer: subject

3. Fischer: subject

4. Couperin: subject

5. Bach: subject

6. Bach: subject

Answers

2. Fischer: answer

3. Fischer: answer

4. Couperin: answer

5. Bach: answer

6. Bach: answer

D. Add episodes and entries to the fugue exposition written in Section C. Continue to pattern the fugue after the Bach Fugue in C minor in the text. Then write a concluding statement that returns to the original key.

Review

1. Look at the list of terms at the head of the chapter (textbook page 47) and provide a definition for each term. Check your definition with that given in the chapter. There are more terms associated with the fugue than many other forms, and you will need a command of the terminology to analyze or discuss its contents.

2. Study Figure 3.10 in the textbook after listening to the fugue. There is a great deal of information about the structure of fugues in the labels on this work. The summary outline on page 60 will give you an overall picture of the form of this work.

3. Listen to other fugues by Bach and see if you can analyze them using the terminology of this chapter. The forty-eight fugues of *The Well-Tempered Clavier* will provide ample works for study.

Test Yourself 3

Answers are on page 228.

1. In the following excerpt from Bach's Fugue in G Major, BWV 561. the subject is given a (real/tonal) answer (circle one). If it is tonal, explain the modification(s) and state the reason for a tonal answer.

Bach: Fugue in G Major, BWV 561.

2. In the excerpt below from Bach's Fugue in E Minor, BWV 551, the subject is given a (real/tonal) answer (circle one). If it is tonal, explain the modification(s) and state the reason for a tonal answer.

Bach: Fugue in E Minor, BWV 551.

3. In the following excerpt from Bach's Fugue in C Minor, BWV 574, the subject is given a (real/tonal) answer (circle one). If it is tonal, explain the modification(s) and state the reason for a tonal answer.

Bach: Fugue in C Minor, BWV 574.

4. Analyze the following fugue of Bach using Figure 3.10 in the textbook (pages 55–59) as a model.

Bach: Fugue in D Minor, BWV 899.

CHAPTER 4
Borrowed Chords

A. The following are four-part chorale phrases.
1. Add alto and tenor according to the figured-bass symbols.
2. Provide a complete harmonic analysis.

1.

6   6
       5
       b

____: __ __ __ __ __ __ __ __
Key

2.

b5   b6   4   6   6
     4   2
____: __ __ __ __ __ __
Key

3.

4   6   6   6   6
3   b
____: __ __ __ __ __ __ __ __ __ __
Key

8.

Key _____: ____ ____ ____ ____   ____ ____ ____

Exercise no. 9 modulates. Blanks are omitted to allow for proper bracketing of the common-chord modulation.

9.

Key _____:

B. Add accidentals to this composition to create borrowed chords. Remember that too many borrowed chords will simply revert the entire composition to the parallel minor mode.

C. Write a short composition of sixteen measures.

1. Use the following form:

Phrase	Phrase Relationship	Key	Cadence
1	a	B♭ major	Half
2	b (contrasting)	B♭ major	Authentic
3	a′	B♭ major	Half
4	b′ (contrasting)	B♭ major	Authentic

2. Use the following chord progressions:

Phrase 1

I   ii°⁶   vii°⁷/V   I$^6_4$ V

Phrase 2

I   ♭VI   ii°⁶   V   I

Phrase 3

I   iv   vii°⁷/V   I$^6_4$ V

Phrase 4

I   vii°⁷   I   V⁷   I

3. Use homophonic texture (melody with chordal accompaniment).
4. Write for any instrument, instruments, or voice as long as the compositions can be performed by class members.
5. Play the composition in class.
6. After it is played as written, replay the composition making all borrowed chords diatonic (remove accidentals). Have the students determine whether they prefer the diatonic chords or the borrowed chords.

D. Following are eight phrases containing only a figured bass. These are similar in type to the chorale phrases in section A, page 15, except that the soprano melody is not provided.

1. Copy the figured bass on a separate sheet of score paper and include a blank staff line above and below it.
2. On a separate staff, write out the notes of the chords in simple position, in accordance with the figured-bass symbols. For phrase 1, your score should look like this:

3. Fashion a suitable soprano melody to accompany the bass melody. If you are not quite sure what a suitable melody is, examine several chorale melodies. Some suggestions follow:

   a. For the time being, use note-for-note values (in this case, mostly quarter notes). Of course, chorale melodies are not made up entirely of quarter notes, but unless you have already had considerable experience, it is better to write conservatively.

   b. Downward (pitch) motion is used more often than upward when approaching a cadence and when the bass voice ascends. Contrary motion between bass and soprano is usually preferred over similar motion and much preferred over parallel motion.

c.   Try at least two or three different soprano melodies before you make a final decision. Choose the one you think is most compatible with the bass line.

d.   As you are writing the soprano melodies, continually check the chords to make sure that the melody notes you have chosen are indeed chord tones. For the moment, each soprano melody note should be consonant with the bass note that sounds with it.

4.   When a suitable soprano melody has been achieved, begin to add the alto and tenor voices. When completed, check again to make sure that all four voices are compatible and that no errors have mysteriously appeared.

5.   Occasionally, the chosen soprano melody may force you to make the voice leading of the alto and tenor voices impossible or, at best, awkward and unmusical. If that unfortunate occurrence should develop, a reworking of the soprano melody is your only choice.

6.   Make a harmonic analysis of each completed four-voice phrase.

E. The following are excerpts contain borrowed chords. Provide a complete harmonic analysis.

1. Bach: "Christus, der ist mein Leben" ("Christ Is My Life"), BWV 281, mm. 5–8.

2. Schumann: "Ich Grolle Nicht" ("I Bear No Grudge") from *Dichterliebe*, op. 48, no. 7, mm. 1–4.

3. Brahms: "Liebesklage des Mädchens" ("The Maiden's Love Lament"), op. 48, no. 3, mm. 11–13.

4. Schumann: *Papillions* (Butterflies), op. 2, no. 5, mm 5–8.

5. Chopin: Mazurka in C Major, op. 33, no. 3, mm. 18–21.

6. Joplin: Maple Leaf Rag, mm. 13–16.

Review

1. Study Figure 4.1 on page 69 of the textbook, particularly the second line, where the most common borrowed chords in major keys are listed. Choose a major key and spell these five borrowed chords. Continue until you can easily spell all of the chords.

2. Study Figures 4.9–4.13 (pages 74–76 of the textbook), which illustrate the most common progressions from each of the borrowed chords in major. Notice that all of the borrowed chords are commonly followed by the dominant chord except the vii°⁷, which is followed by the tonic chord. Choose a major key and practice writing each of the borrowed chords in four parts and resolving it to the dominant chord or tonic as appropriate. Continue practicing in various keys until you can easily resolve any of the common borrowed chords in major.

3. Play each of the progressions you have written in number 2 above to familiarize yourself with the musical effect of the borrowed chords.

Test Yourself 4

Answers are on page 230.

The following are examples of the five most common borrowed chords, from minor keys to major keys.

1. Analyze the borrowed chord. Analysis can be effected by determining the chord type (ii° is a diminished triad, ii⁰⁷ is a diminished-minor 7th chord, iv is a minor triad, ♭VI is a major triad, and vii°⁷ is a diminished-diminished 7th chord).

2. Name the key in which the example functions as a *borrowed* chord.

3. Write the chord that normally follows the given chord in four-part harmony.

4. Provide a Roman numeral analysis for both chords.

CHAPTER 5
Neapolitan 6th Chords

A. Complete the following voice-leading exercises. Note that some of the later phrases contain a modulation.

   1. Add tenor and alto to the figured-bass chorale phrases.

   2. Provide a complete harmonic analysis of each phrase.

1.

2.

3.

4.

5.

6.

7.

8.

9.

10.

11.

B. Following are eight phrases containing only a figured bass. These are similar in type to the assignment in Chapter 4, Section D, page 18.

1. Compose an appropriate soprano melody for each of the phrases.
2. Fill in the alto and tenor voices.
3. Make a complete harmonic analysis of each phrase.

C. Following are three chorale melodies.
1. List the three possible triads that can be used to support each quarter note.
2. Harmonize the melody on scratch paper using only root-position diatonic triads in block style.
3. Substitute secondary dominants, Neapolitan 6th chords, and other altered chords for some of the triads.
4. Sketch in a bass line that has sufficient contrary motion to the melody and contains an appropriate contour.
5. Add the remaining voices using recommended part-writing procedures.
6. Add nonharmonic tones where appropriate.
7. Make a complete harmonic analysis of your composition.

D. The following (example a) is a short, four-voice composition. Making this the basis for another composition:
1. Complete the composition (at b).
2. Continue the figure as shown in the first two measures.
3. Place the figure in any voice.
4. Use one chord per measure throughout until you reach the final chord.
5. Expand the final chord into two measures.
6. Make a complete harmonic analysis.
7. Add tempo markings.
8. Add all necessary marks for interpretation.

E. The following are excerpts from songs by Schubert and Haydn. Provide a complete harmonic analysis.

1. Schubert: "Der Müller und der Bach" ("The Miller and the Brook") from *Die Schöne Müllerin* (The Miller's Beautiful Daughter), op. 25, no. 19, D. 795, mm. 1–28.

seh'n;_____ da hal - ten die Eng - lein die Au - gen sich zu und

schluch - zen und sin - gen die See - le zur Ruh! Und

2. Haydn: "Lob der Faulheit" ("Praise of Idleness"), Hob. XXVIa:22, mm. 18–33.

mir, dich nach Wür - den, dich nach Wür - den zu be -

sin - - - gen! Doch ich will mein Best - es tun:

nach der Ar - beit ist gut ruh'n.

Review

1. Select a major triad and name the keys in which it would be the Neapolitan 6th chord (both major and minor). Continue practicing until you can quickly name the key.

2. Turn to the circle of fifths (Figure 2.20 on page 38 of volume 1). For each key spell the Neapolitan 6th chord.

3. Study Figure 5.10 on page 88 of the textbook, which illustrates proper voice leading for the Neapolitan 6th chord. Practice writing and resolving the N^6 chord in a variety of major and minor keys, using Figure 5.10 as a guide. Pay particular attention to example e, which shows the way to avoid parallel 5ths in resolving the Neapolitan 6th to the tonic six-four.

Test Yourself 5

Answers are on page 231.

A. Each given triad in four-part harmony is the V chord in a minor key.
1. Determine the key (minor), and write it in the blank provided.
2. Determine the Neapolitan 6th chord in this key, and write it in four-part harmony so that it leads smoothly to the V triad.
3. Place the analysis beneath each chord (see measure 1 for an example).

a: N⁶   V

____ : ____ ____   ____ : ____ ____   ____ : ____ ____
Key   Key   Key

B. Complete in the same manner as A. The vii°⁷/V is added between the N⁶ and the V triad (see measure 5 for an example).

f: N⁶   vii°⁷/V   V

____ : ___ ___ ___   ____ : ___ ___ ___   ____ : ___ ___ ___
Key   Key   Key

C. Complete in the same manner as A. The i_4^6 chord is added between the N⁶ and the V triad (see measure 9 for an example).

c: N⁶ i_4^6 V

____ : ___ ___ ___   ____ : ___ ___ ___   ____ : ___ ___ ___
Key   Key   Key

CHAPTER 6
Augmented 6th Chords

A. Write an Italian augmented 6th chord above each given tone. Use the most conventional position of the chord. The given tone is the lowest note of the chord.

B. Write an German augmented 6th chord above each given tone. Use the most conventional position of the chord.

C. Write an French augmented 6th chord above each given tone. Use the most conventional position of the chord.

D. Complete the following exercises in the following manner:
1. Add tenor and alto to the figured-bass chorale phrases.
2. Make an analysis of each chord.

34   PART B   Chromatic Harmony

7.

8.

9.

10.

E. The following eight phrases contain only a figured bass. These are similar in type to the assignments in Chapter 4, Section D (page 18), and Chapter 5, Section B (page 26).
1. Compose an appropriate soprano melody for each of the phrases.
2. Fill in the alto and tenor voices.
3. Make a complete harmonic analysis of each phrase.

F. The four short excerpts shown here contain augmented 6th chords. Provide a complete harmonic analysis of each. Excerpt 1 illustrates conventional treatment.

1. Beethoven: Bagatelle in G Minor, op. 119, no. 1, mm. 9–16.

Excerpt 2 contains one example in which an augmented 6th chord includes a nonharmonic upper pedal tune.

2. Schubert: Sonata in A Minor, op. 42, D. 845, mm. 1–10.

Can you account for the spelling of the augmented 6th chord in excerpt 3?

3. Schumann: *Drei Stücklein* (Three Pieces), III, from *Bunte Blätter* (Multicolored Leaves), op. 99, no. 3, mm. 1–8.

In excerpt 4, augmented 6th chords are given traditional treatment, but measures 5–7 contain some curious modal mixtures.

4. Schubert: "Die Liebe hat gelogen" ("The Love Has Lied"), op. 23, no. 1, D. 751, mm. 1–7.

G. Analyze the following excerpt from a Beethoven string quartet.
1. Provide a complete harmonic analysis.
2. Are the augmented 6th chords employed conventionally?
3. How does the spacing of instruments in this composition compare with that of the baroque four-part chorales?
4. Review the range of each of the instruments used in a string quartet.

Beethoven: String Quartet in C Minor, op. 18, no. 4, IV, mm. 1–16.

H. Refer to Schumann's *Davidsbündlesrtänze*, op. 6, no. 8 on page 215.
  1. Make a complete harmonic analysis of this composition.
  2. Determine if the chromatic chords receive traditional treatment in their spelling, position, and resolution.
  3. For the purpose of review, identify the cadences, phrases, and form of the work.
  4. Listen as a member of the class plays the excerpt. Discuss your aural perception of the chromatic chords.

Review

1. Study Figure 6.3 on page 98 of the textbook, which shows the three common notes among the augmented 6th chords. Practice writing the common notes above various notes, and then add the extra tones to create the Gr⁶ and Fr⁶ in each case. Identify the major or minor key where you would likely find each chord.
2. Turn to the circle of fifths (Figure 2.20 on page 38 of volume 1) and spell the three augmented 6th chords in each key. Write each chord in four-part harmony, and resolve the augmented 6th in the most conventional way (outward to an octave). Fill in the remaining voices to spell the dominant chord (or the tonic six-four in the case of the Gr⁶). Study Figures 6.16–6.18 on pages 104–105 of the text for proper voice-leading procedures.
3. The Gr⁶ chord is spelled enharmonically in major keys (study Figure 6.18). Check your work in number 2 above to make sure that the Gr⁶ chord is correctly spelled in major keys. If not, change the spelling to avoid chromatic resolution of the 5th above the bass in the Gr⁶ chord.

Test Yourself 6

Answers are on page 231.

Each of the following chords is an augmented 6th chord in four-part harmony. Identify and label the augmented 6th chord (It⁶, Gr⁶, or Fr⁶). Identify the key(s) in which the particular augmented 6th chord is most often found. Write a chord that represents the most conventional resolution of the given chord in four parts, using proper voice leading. Analyze the resolution chord.

CHAPTER 7
Variation Technique

A. The following excerpts are from works that have been composed using variation techniques.
   1. Have a pianist play each of the excerpts in class.
   2. Make a complete harmonic analysis.
   3. On the scores themselves, circle nonharmonic tones and name the type (abbreviate or use initials).
   4. Discuss:
      a. The variation techniques used by each composer. Indicate whether each variation is essentially melodic, harmonic, rhythmic, contrapuntal, etc., or a combination of techniques.
      b. The type of variation form—*continuous variation* or *theme and variation.*
      c. The relationship of each variation to the original theme.
   5. Arrange some of the excerpts for instruments played by class members and perform them.

1. Brahms: Chaconne after J. S. Bach (BWV 1016) from *Five Studies for the Piano.*

2. Bach: Aria with Thirty Variations ("Goldberg" Variations), BWV 988, mm. 1–16.

Variatio 1

Variatio 3
Canone all' Unisono

Variatio 7

Variatio 10
Fughetta

Variatio 18
Canone alla Sesta

3. Buxtehude: Ciacona in C Minor, BuxWV 159, mm. 1–29.

4. Beethoven: Thirty-two Variations on an Original Theme in C Minor for Piano, WoO 80.

Var. I

Var. IX
con espressione

Var. XII
Maggiore

Var. XVIII

Var. XXII

Var. XXX

B. Refer to Robert Schumann's Theme with Variations from *Drei Clavier-Sonaten für die Jugend*, op. 118, no. 1, on page 217.

1. Listen to a performance or a recording of this composition.
2. Make a complete harmonic, melodic, and formal analysis of the work.
3. Assess the following:
    a. The variation techniques used by Schumann.
    b. The type of variation form—*continuous variation* or *theme and variation.*
    c. The relationship of each variation to the original theme.
4. Write a short paper of 200–400 words summarizing the findings of your analysis.
    a. Describe how circle progressions, modulations, and key relationships shape the harmonic flow of the composition.
    b. Include information about cadences, phrases, and the form.
    c. Write about your findings concerning variation techniques.
    d. Indicate any other items you think are interesting.

Review

1. This chapter presents two types of variations:
    a. continuous variations
    b. theme and variations
    Read the short sections on pages 117–119 that describe each type. Make sure that you understand the differences between them.
2. Study the variation techniques discussed on pages 120–124, paying particular attention to the musical examples. For your convenience, the techniques are listed on page 124 of the textbook.
3. Theme and variation movements abound in the classical and romantic periods. Listen to a number of such movements, and try to identify instances of each of the variation techniques.

Test Yourself 7

Answers are on page 232.

The instructions below refer to excerpts from Mozart's variations on the familiar tune, "Twinkle, Twinkle Little Star" (Variations on "Ah, vous dirai-je, Maman," K. 265). The first section of the theme is stated below:

1. For each of the variation excerpts that follow, identify the theme by circling the notes of the original melody.
2. Identify the variation technique(s) employed in each variation, referring to the list of variation techniques on page 124 of the textbook. Some variations contain more than one technique.

Mozart: Variations on "Ah, vous dirai-je, Maman" (Ah, Shall I tell You, Mama), K. 265, mm. 1–8.

Variation technique(s) in Variation I: _____

Variation technique(s) in Variation II: _____

Var. V

Variation technique(s) in Variation V: _____

Var. VII

Variation technique(s) in Variation VII: _____

Var. VIII
Minore

Variation technique(s) in Variation VIII: _____

Var. XI
Adagio

Variation technique(s) in Variation XI: _____

Var. XII
Allegro

Variation technique(s) in Variation XII: _____

CHAPTER 8
Sonata Form

A. Refer to page 194 to make a complete analysis of Mozart's Piano Sonata in G Major, K. 283 (I: Allegro). Use as a model the analysis found in Chapter 8 of the textbook. The form of this sonata movement is fairly traditional, but the following suggestions will assist in understanding some slight departures.

1. While the material in most development sections can be traced easily to first theme, second theme, transitions, etc., deriving the source of material in this development is somewhat more difficult. The development, quite short by most standards, begins with carefully camouflaged characteristics of theme 1 (first theme of the exposition).

2. This movement contains some excellent examples of linear progressions. The normal stream of circle progressions is occasionally interrupted for what may be described as melodic (or linear) priorities. The following excerpt from this movement is an excellent example. Note how the harmony moves in parallel lockstep with the melody and ceases to create definite chord progressions. In measure 47, strong harmonic progressions (ii–V^7–I) are temporarily restored but then lapse again into linear movement (measure 48).

3. Other examples of linear progressions occur in measures 16–21, 83–88, 111–113, and 115–116.

4. Measures 34, 39, 101, and 106 contain harmony that changes every eighth note. While analyzing each chord may provide good practice, other approaches might explain the nature of these measures more precisely.

61

B. Refer to Haydn's Piano Sonata in G Major, Hob. XVI:27 (I: Allegro con brio), on page 179. Use as a model the analysis found in Chapter 8 of the textbook. Some problems are as follows:

1. *Possible overlapping phrases.* Melodically, some phrases are constructed to lead directly to the next without pause. An example is at measures 35–36. One interpretation, based on harmonic influence (V to I), would consider the first beat of measure 36 as an overlap—both the end of the concluding phrase and the beginning of the next. Another interpretation, based strictly on the melodic content, would consider that the concluding phrase ends on the last beat of measure 35, and the new one begins on the first beat of measure 36—thus no overlap. Both interpretations have merit.

2. *Determining phrase lengths.* In this movement, the frequent lack of a melodic hiatus creates difficulty in determining the length of phrases. For example, are measures 13–24 comprised of one or two phrases? Melodic content might suggest two (measures 13–16 and 17–24), whereas the lack of a melodic hiatus and absence of a strong cadence would imply only one.

3. *Content of the development section.* Although the restless nature of the development is preserved in this section, the origin of the melodic content may prove more difficult to determine.

4. *Content of the recapitulation.* Do not assume that the recapitulation is simply a rewrite (in the tonic key) of the exposition.

C. Following the same procedures outlined in Chapter 8 of the textbook, analyze Beethoven's Piano Sonata in G Major, op. 14, no. 2 (I: Allegro), on page 141.

Review

1. Study the brief outline of a standard sonata form on page 135 of the textbook.
2. Study the description of the sections of a sonata form on pages 136–141. For each section compare the description to the corresponding section in the Mozart sonata movement analyzed in Figure 8.7. You can use this analysis as a model for your own analysis of sonata movements.
3. The first movement of most classical period sonatas, string quartets, and symphonies is in sonata form. Listen to a number of such works, and try to identify the following factors:

    I. Exposition
        a. First theme
        b. Transition
        c. Second theme
        d. Third (closing) theme
        e. Codetta

    II. Development
        a. Appearance of themes 1 and 2
        b. Retransition

    III. Recapitulation
        a. First theme
        b. Transition
        c. Second theme
        d. Third (closing) theme
        e. Coda

You may not find all the elements listed in the outline, and some movements may contain additional elements such as introductions and new themes in the development.

Test Yourself 8

Answers are on page 235.

The following questions refer to the Clementi Sonatina movement that follows. The term *sonatina* is the diminutive of sonata and is often applied to brief works in the form. Some sonatina movements have little or no development section, but this example, in spite of its extreme brevity, is perfectly proportioned.

1. Do a Roman numeral analysis or macro analysis of the entire movement.

2. The exposition section is from measure 1 to measure _____.

3. The "development" section is from measure _____ to measure _____.

4. The recapitulation section is from measure _____ to measure _____.

5. The first theme is _____ measures in length.

6. The transition between the first and second themes is _____ measures in length.

7. The second theme is _____ measures in length.

8. The "development" is based on the _____ theme.

9. How does the recapitulation differ from the exposition?

Clementi: Sonatina in C Major, op. 36, no. 1, I.

PART C   The Classical Period

CHAPTER 9
Rondo Forms

A. Refer to Beethoven's Piano Sonata in G Major, op. 49, no. 2 (II: Tempo di Menuetto), on page 150. After listening to this composition, make a complete harmonic analysis. Then, on a separate sheet of paper:

1. Prepare a chart displaying the phrase-by-phrase analysis of the form.

2. As a part of the chart, show how the overall form is created from the phrase-by-phrase analysis.

3. Write a short paper of 200 to 400 words specifying information you learned from your analysis. Here are some ideas to help you get started. Indicate:

    a. How the key relationships help to solidify the form of the movement.

    b. Phrase lengths—generally similar or dissimilar in length.

    c. Smaller forms within the overall form. Do phrases combine to form periods? Do periods combine to form double periods? Are any sections of the movement complete in themselves?

    d. Any aspects of the form that depart from textbook descriptions.

    e. Any harmony or harmonic progressions that were difficult for you to analyze. What about measures 9 and 10? Measures 42–46?

    f. Any recurring melodic, harmonic, nonharmonic (such as pedal tones), or rhythmic features that tend to unify the work.

    g. Compare general characteristics of this movement with others you have analyzed.

B. Refer to Haydn's Piano Sonata in D Major, Hob. XVI:19 (III: Allegro assai), found on page 174. Complete the analysis of this movement following the same directions as found in Section A above.

C. Refer to Beethoven's Piano Sonata in C Minor *(Pathétique),* op. 13 (II: Adagio cantabile), on page 136. Make an analysis using the same directions as in Section A and compare the movement by Beethoven with the rondo in D major by Haydn (see Section B).

D. Write the first three sections of a five-part rondo form using the harmonic and melodic vocabulary of the late eighteenth century (classical period). Model the form after the first three sections (A B A) of the rondo in Piano Sonata in D Major by Haydn on page 174.

1. Write for the piano or any small group of instruments that are played by class members.

2. Use any of the following five melodies in any combination you wish (you will need two). You will probably need to transpose them to fit the key relationships of the model.

3. If you wish, you may compose your own melodies, but be sure to show them to the instructor before proceeding with the composition.

4. Play the composition in class and have the students determine the overall form as well as the form of the various smaller sections.

E. Complete the remaining two sections of the five-part rondo begun in Section D. Continue to model your composition after the rondo in D major by Haydn.

Play the completed composition in class. Have the class members choose some of the better works and schedule them for a student recital.

Review

1. Review the outlines of the three-part, five-part, and seven-part rondos on pages 165–166 of the text.
2. Examine Figures 9.1–9.6 on pages 167–172 in the textbook in detail, along with the summary discussion that follows. The rondo forms are very straightforward. The basic idea is that a single theme (called a refrain) is repeated a number of times, interspersed with contrasting materials (called episodes). Any composition with these properties can be called a rondo.

Test Yourself 9

Answers are on page 237.

The instructions below refer to the third movement from Clementi's Sonatina No. 5 in G Major, which follows on the next page. This work, in spite of its extreme brevity, is a complete seven-part rondo.

1. Do a Roman numeral analysis or macro analysis of the movement.
2. Identify the refrain (the A theme). The key will be important in determining the length of the theme.
3. Make an outline of the form. Include any transitions, retransitions, codettas, and coda in your outline.

Clementi: Sonatina in G Major, op. 36, no. 5, III: Rondo.

Allegro di molto

CHAPTER 10
9th, 11th, and 13th Chords

A. Write the requested chord above each given note. The examples illustrate correct procedure.

1. Write a MmM 9th chord above each note (see measure 1 for an example).

2. Write a Mmm 9th chord above each note (see measure 11 for an example).

3. Write a dominant 11th chord above each note (see measure 21 for an example).

4. Write a dominant 11th chord with augmented 11th above each note (see measure 31 for an example).

5. Write a dominant 13th chord above each note (see measure 41 for an example).

B. Reharmonize a popular song of your choosing.
   1. Select a popular song with which you are very familiar.
   2. On a separate sheet of paper, rewrite the melody line and the popular music chord symbols.
   3. Play over the melody several times using block chords and the popular music chord symbols given.
   4. Experiment with the harmony by keeping the basic chords as given, but make them into 9th, 11th, or 13th chords whenever the effect is desirable.
   5. When you have made your final selection of 9th, 11th, and 13th chords, change the block chords into a suitable accompaniment pattern for any instrument or group of instruments that can assure a performance in class.
   6. Perform the revised compositions in class. Have a voice major sing the melody line while accompanied by the instrument(s) of your choice.

C. Write a composition in rounded binary (incipient three-part) form.
   1. Employ the following formal design:

Phrase	Key	Cadence	Relationship	Larger Form
1	B♭ major	Half	a	A
2	B♭ major modulating to F major	Authentic in F major	ap (parallel)	
3	F major modulating back to B♭ major	Half in B♭ major	b	B
4	B♭ major	Authentic	a′	A′

   2. Arrange the harmonic vocabulary to contain no simple triads. Suggested chords are:
      a. 9th chords
      b. 11th chords
      c. 13th chords
      d. 7th chords (any kind)
   3. Write for any instrument or instruments played by class members.
   4. Perform the compositions in class. Have the class select the best composition for a performance in a student recital.

D. Harmonize the following folk song melodies. Procedures for harmonizing melodies are outlined in volume 1 of the textbook in Chapter 10.
   1. Play or sing the following melodies until you are entirely familiar with them before beginning the exercises.
   2. Experiment with simple triadic harmony at the piano. At this point, play only block chords.
   3. On a separate sheet of paper, rewrite the melody and add the block harmony you think fits best.
   4. Add factors (7ths, 9ths, 11ths, and/or 13ths) to some of the existing chords, examining those that might add additional color to the accompaniment.
   5. Plan the accompaniment for a guitar, a piano, or an instrumental combo.
   6. With the block chords (now containing additional factors) as a basis, fashion an accompaniment pattern appropriate to the instrument(s) you selected.
   7. Write words of your own for each of the melodies. Place the words in the form of a *ballad* (a simple narrative poem made up of stanzas), one stanza for the sixteen measures printed. The same music is repeated for each stanza.
   8. Perform the works in class.

1. Folk Song: "Barbara Allen."

2. Folk Song: "Rising Sun."

E. Use suggested part-writing procedures discussed in the text.
1. Write from the figured bass the remaining three voices of each chord.
2. Name the key of each exercise.
3. Write the analysis of each chord in the blanks provided.

F. Following are five phrases.

    1. Add the alto and tenor voices according to the figured-bass or chord symbols.

    2. Make an analysis of each chord.

    3. Concerning these exercises:

       a. Numbers 1–3 contain figured-bass symbols, while in numbers 4 and 5, chord symbols are given.

       b. Generally, when 9th, 11th, or 13th chords are called for, the figured-bass includes directions for all three voices above the bass. In a few instances (as in number 1, chord 4), the missing factor is the interval of a diatonic 3rd above the bass.

       c. Note that in numbers 4 and 5, all symbols for 9th and 13th chords call for dominant (or secondary dominant) chords. As an example, the "C#13" refers to a C# dominant 13th chord, the "F#9" indicates an F# dominant 9th, and so on. Make sure that you add whatever accidentals are needed to create the dominant sound.

       d. For number 4, it is suggested that the entire phrase be analyzed in the key of G major.

1.

2.

3.

4.

5.

G. On the next page are three short melodies excerpted from popular songs by Duke Ellington.
1. Copy the melodies on score paper leaving three blank staves below each system of melody.
2. On the lowest (4th) staff, write out the chords in simple (closest) position.
3. On the two middle staves, compose a piano accompaniment.
   a. In the piano accompaniment, it is sometimes necessary (and desirable) to use chords in inversion for a smooth bass line and better voice leading.
   b. Because many of the chords are thick textured, it is wise to omit factors that would create excess dissonance and dense sonorities.
   c. The following illustrates one example of the first line of number 1:

Ellington: "Come Sunday."

4. Regarding the circled numbers above the chord symbols:

a. At number 1, the soprano (D) creates a 13th above the root (F), but the chord symbol calls for a dominant sounding 7th chord only.

b. Similarly at number 2, the soprano (A) creates an 11th above the root (E♭), but the chord symbol calls for a dominant-sounding 9th chord.

c. At numbers 3, 4, and 5, the bass note in the final two measures of the accompaniment should be B♭. E♭/B♭ (no. 3) means to play an E♭ major triad with B♭ as the bass note. Likewise, at number 4, the bass note should retain the B♭. The B♭⁶ at number 5 means to play a B♭ major triad with an added sixth (G).

d. At number 6, the melody note (G♯) is enharmonic with the chord symbol A♭7. Apparently, the composer considered A♭7 to be simpler than G♯7.

e. At number 7, the chord symbol is standard for a 13th chord with a minor 13th.

f. At number 8, although the composer requests an A♭13, be careful how you employ the 13th in your accompaniment—avoid an excessively dissonant clash with the melody note.

1. Ellington: "Come Sunday."

2. Ellington: "Doin' the Crazy Walk."

3. Ellington: "Lady in Blue."

H. Following are two short excerpts by Duke Ellington. Make a complete analysis of each.

1. Both excerpts abound in circle progressions and contain both 9th and 13th chords.

2. In "I Got It Bad," the circle progressions are clear and easy to identify. The final chord (measure 8b) is a major triad with an added 6th—the root is G.

3. In "Echoes of Harlem," measure 4 (which is repeated in measure 12) is an enigma. The chord (G♭, B♭, D♭, F♭ [enharmonic with E]) is a tritone substitute for C, E, G, B♭ and may be analyzed in at least two ways. An A♭ major triad with an added 6th can be found in measures 8 and 18.

1. Ellington: "I Got It Bad."

2. Ellington: "Echos of Harlem."

Review

1. Spell the dominant 9th, 11th, and 13th chords in all major and minor keys. (Note that the 9th and 13th are major in the major keys and minor in the minor keys.)
2. Study Figure 10.1 on page 181 of the textbook. Memorize the most common factors present in four-part settings of these chords and the voice-leading guides for each chord. Write dominant 9th, 11th, and 13th chords in a number of major and minor keys in four-part harmony and resolve each to its respective tonic triad using figure 10.12 as a guide.
3. If your instructor indicates that you should know the popular music chords symbols for the various 9th, 11th, and 13th chord qualities, study Appendix C on page 359 of the textbook by playing each chord on the piano and transposing that chord to different roots. Pay particular attention to the popular music chord symbol for each chord.

Test Yourself 10

Answers are on page 241.

All the following chords are secondary dominant 9th, 11th, or 13th chords.
1. Analyze each chord as a secondary dominant in two different keys and write the analysis in the blanks provided.
2. The example illustrates the correct procedure.

B: V^9/V ____ ____ ____ ____ ____ ____ ____ ____ ____

E: V^9/ii ____ ____ ____ ____ ____ ____ ____ ____ ____

CHAPTER 11
Altered Dominants

A. Each of the following chords is an altered dominant.
   1. Write the correct analysis on the first blank beneath the staff.
   2. Write the name of the key on the second blank beneath the staff.
   3. The example illustrates the correct procedure.

V⁺⁷ → V^{+7}

G

B. Each of the following tones represents the root of the altered dominant named directly beneath it.
   1. On the staff, write the remaining tones of the requested chord.
   2. The example illustrates the correct procedure.

V^+ $V^7_{5\flat}$ $v^{ø7}$ V^{+7} $V^{5\flat}$ V^{+7} $V^{5\flat}$ $v^{ø7}$ V^+ $V^7_{5\natural}$

C. Altered dominants can occur also as secondary altered dominants. Following are the keys and analysis symbols for ten such chords.
   1. Write the requested secondary altered dominant on the staff in the blank measure provided.
   2. The example illustrates the correct procedure.

A: V^+/V B♭: $V^{5\flat}/V$ E: $v^{ø7}/V$ G: V^{+7}/V C: $V^7_{5\flat}/V$

F: V^+/IV d: $V^{5\flat}/VI$ D: $v^{ø7}/IV$ g: V^{+7}/VI B: $V^7_{5\flat}/IV$

D. Add the alto and tenor voices, and provide a harmonic analysis of each chord.

1.

2.

3.

4.

5.

E. Following are five phrases containing only a figured bass. These are similar in type to the assignment in Chapter 4, Section D, page 18.

1. Compose an appropriate soprano melody for each of the phrases.
2. Fill in the alto and tenor voices.
3. Make a complete harmonic analysis of each phrase.

F. Have a member of the class who is a piano major play the following excerpt.

1. Do a Roman numeral analysis and/or macro analysis of this excerpt.

2. Discuss the use of altered dominants in the composition.

3. Discuss the form of the work.

4. Have one member of the class arrange the composition for four instruments played by class members. Play the work in class.

5. Have those members who are not playing instruments sing the excerpt on a syllable such as *la, lu,* or *ta,* taking out-of-range tones up or down an octave as the need arises.

Beethoven: Bagatelle in C Major, op. 119, no. 8.

G. Compose the first sixteen measures of a popular song.

   1. Use the following progressions or make up your own. If you decide to compose your own progressions, be sure to use a generous number of altered dominants.

Upbeat:	G^{+7}					
Measures 1:	C	C$\sharp^{\circ7}$	Measures 9:	C	C$\sharp^{\circ7}$	
2:	D$_{MI}^7$	D$\sharp^{\circ7}$	10:	D$_{MI}^7$	D$\sharp^{\circ7}$	
3:	E$_{MI}^7$		11:	E$_{MI}^7$		
4:	A^7		12:	A^7		
5:	D$_{MI}^7$	G^7	13:	D$_{MI}^7$	G^7	
6:	C		14:	C	E$_{MI}^7$	A^7
7:	G$_{MI}^7$	A^7	15:	D$_{MI}^7$	G^{+7}	
8:	D$_{MI}^7$	G^7 G^{+7}	16:	C^6		

   2. After selecting the progressions, write a melody to accompany.
   3. Write your own lyrics to the song.
   4. The accompaniment to the melody may be written for piano, guitar, or instrumental combo.
   5. Arrange the block chords into an appropriate accompaniment figure.
   6. Have a voice major sing the melodies with appropriate accompaniment in class.

H. Following is a blues melody with chord symbols by Thelonious Monk.
   1. Make a complete harmonic analysis of the composition.
   2. Determine which chord symbols represent primary and secondary dominants.
   3. Based on your findings, experiment with altering the dominants. You may need to write out the chords in simple (closest) position to determine which notes can be altered successfully.
   4. On a separate sheet of score paper, write out the melody and add your set of modified chord symbols.
   5. Have a jazz combo perform the harmonizations in class. Discuss which arrangements incorporate altered dominants most successfully.

Thelonious Monk (transcribed by Steve Cardenas): *Blue Monk.*

Review

1. Study Figure 11.1 (page 195 of the textbook), which shows the five altered dominant chords in common use. Choose a major key, spell the dominant 7th chord, and then alter it to make each of the five chords illustrated in Figure 11.1. Repeat this process in several other keys.

2. Study Figure 11.7, which shows proper voice leading of altered dominant chords. Write each of the chords you spelled in number 1 above in four parts and resolve them properly to the tonic chord. Use the section titled "Voice Leading" on page 199 for advice in proper voice leading.

Test Yourself 11

Answers are on page 242.

Each of the following chords falls into one or more of the categories listed below.
1. Identify each chord using the letters *a, b, c, d, e,* or *f* from the list. If a chord fits more than one category, give a letter for each category.
2. The example illustrates the proper procedure (see measure 1).

Categories:
a. 9th, 11th, or 13th chord
b. Neapolitan 6th chord
c. Augmented 6th chord
d. Altered dominant
e. Borrowed chord
f. Secondary dominant or leading-tone chord

CHAPTER 12
Chromatic Mediants

A. Write each of the six chromatic mediants in the following keys. The example illustrates the correct procedure.

1. (Ex.)

D major: III   ♮III   ♮iii   VI   ♭VI   ♭vi

2. B♭ major:

3. F minor:

4. E major:

5. D♭ major:

6. C♯ minor:

7. G minor:

B. Add the alto and tenor voices, and provide a harmonic analysis.

1.

2.

3.

4.

C. Following are five phrases containing only a figured bass. These are similar in type to the assignment in Chapter 4, Section D, page 18.

1. Compose an appropriate soprano melody for each of the phrases.
2. Fill in the alto and tenor voices.
3. Make a complete harmonic analysis of each phrase.

D. Except for the first excerpt, each of the following melodies is a folk song.

1. Using the procedures outlined in volume 1 of the textbook (Chapter 10), harmonize the melodies, including at least one or two chromatic mediants in each.

2. Experiment by trying a fast (rapid change of chords), medium, and slow harmonic rhythm. Then select the one you prefer for each melody.

3. Write the accompaniment for guitar if the class has a guitar player. If the class has none, write for piano or small instrumental combo.

4. Write words of your own to each melody.

5. From the block chords of your original harmonization, fashion an accompaniment that fits the medium you choose (whether guitar, piano, or instrumental combo).

6. Perform the compositions in class. Have a vocal major sing the melodies.

1.

2. Folk Song.

3. Folk Song: Newfoundland.

4. Folk Song: Kentucky.

E. The concluding measures from two compositions by Franz Liszt follow.

   1.   Have a piano major play both of the excerpts in class.

   2.   Make a complete harmonic analysis of the chords.

   3.   Discuss the use of chromatic mediants in each excerpt.

1. Liszt: *Apparitions* no. 2, S. 155, mm. 90–98.

2. Liszt: *Un Sospiro* (A Sigh), no. 3 from *Trois Etudes de Concert* (Three Concert Etudes), S. 144, mm. 66–77.

F. Write a short original composition of two to four phrases.
1. Each phrase should be approximately four measures in length.
2. Use only the harmonic vocabulary studied to date.
3. Employ the following set of chord progressions or make up your own:

G: I ♭VI ♭III I N⁶ V⁷ I ♭VI I III I iv I

If you compose your own harmony, be sure you employ a generous number of chromatic mediants.
4. Write for any group of instruments played by class members.
5. Perform the compositions in class. Have the class critique each composition.

Review

1. Study Figure 12.1 (page 205 of the textbook), which illustrates the six chromatic mediants in the major keys and the minor keys (G major and E minor in the example). Choose a major key and spell all six chromatic mediant chords. Choose a minor key and spell the six chromatic mediant chords. Repeat this process in several other major and minor keys.

2. Chromatic mediants are most often approached or left by root motion of a 3rd, with chromatic motion in one or more parts. Study Figure 12.9 (page 210) to see these characteristics. Figure 12.2 (page 206) illustrates the difference in function of the major triad on the 6th scale degree in major, which may be a secondary dominant of ii or a chromatic mediant, depending on the context. Study this example carefully. Can a similar situation exist with any of the other chromatic mediant chords?

Test Yourself 12

Answers are on page 242.

Write each of the six chromatic mediants in the following keys. The example in Section 12A (page 85) illustrates the correct procedure.

1.

F major:

2.

Bb minor:

3.

F# major:

4.

Ab major:

5.

E minor:

CHAPTER 13
The Romantic Period

A. Refer to Schubert's "Morgengrüss," op. 89, no. 15, D. 975, on page 212. Have a voice major sing the composition.
1. Make a complete harmonic analysis of the chords.
2. On the score itself, circle all nonharmonic tones and name the type.
3. Discuss the following:
    a. The chromatic chords and their treatment
    b. The harmonic rhythm—whether regular, irregular, fast, slow, etc.
4. Arrange the accompaniment of the song for three or four instruments played by class members, and perform the work in class with a vocalist singing the vocal line.

B. Write a short *lied* of your own.
1. Pattern the form and length after Schubert's "Morgengrüss."
2. Be sure to include modal mixture in the composition and incorporate at least two chromatic chords.
3. Either make up words of your own or select a short poem you particularly like.
4. Perform the composition in class with a voice major singing the vocal line.

C. Refer to the partsong, "Sweet and Low," by Joseph Barnby on page 135.
1. Analyze this composition using the strategy suggested for Section A above.
2. Discuss the use of chromatic chords. Assess the common-tone diminished 7th chords appearing in the work.
3. Have the entire class sing this choral composition in class.

D. Have a piano major play each of the following excerpts in class. Make a complete harmonic analysis of each excerpt.

1. Mendelssohn: Sonata in G Minor, op. 105, II, mm. 1–12.

2. Tchaikovsky: *The Nurse's Tale* from *Album for the Young*, op. 39, no. 19, mm. 33–48.

3. Franck: Chorale from the *Prelude, Chorale, and Fugue for Piano*, mm. 1–11.

E. The following excerpt is the development section of a sonatina. Analyze the excerpt, noting the following features:

1. In a few instances, weak key centers are established without reaching a tonic chord—dominant 7th chords are the only evidence of the new tonal center.

2. The excerpt contains no less than eight augmented 6th chords—some are repetitions.

3. Occasionally, an augmented 6th chord occurs in a nonconventional position, creating a diminished 3rd (the inversion of an augmented 6th).

4. Look carefully for upper pedal tones that are employed now and then. Such tones are not to be analyzed as components of the chords.

Schubert: Sonatina for Violin and Piano, op. 137, no. 2, D. 385.

F. Refer to Schubert's "Die Krahe" ("The Crow") from *Winterreise* (Winter Journey), op. 89, no. 15, D. 911, on page 207. Make a complete harmonic analysis of this composition.
    1. Discuss:
        a. The key scheme
        b. The form
        c. The number of phrases
        d. The cadence formulas
        e. Compositional devices such as sequences, repetition, etc.
        f. Harmonic rhythm
        g. Any other significant points regarding this composition
    2. Have two students in the class perform the work, and then discuss pertinent items pertaining to interpretation and performance.

G. Refer to Chopin's Etude, op. 10, no. 2, on page 155. Listen to a recording of this work until you are familiar with it. This composition exhibits a steady stream of chromatic material, most of which is decoration.
    1. Analyze the underlying harmonic material, then compare the chords with the chromatic line above.
    2. Discuss the relationship between the two elements. Does the line always "fit" with the chords?
    3. Divide the work into phrases. What creates the sense of phrasing in this work?
    4. What elements of the romantic style are present in this work?
    5. Write a short analytical paper presenting the results of your analysis.

Review

1. Study Figures 13.10 and 13.11 (page 223 of the textbook) and observe the enharmonic spelling of the diminished 7th chords. Write out four resolutions of chords "B" in Figure 13.10, using Figure 13.11 as a model. Now do the same for chord "C" in Figure 13.10.
2. Select a major or minor key. Spell the dominant 7th chord in that key. Now respell the same chord enharmonically as a German 6th chord (only the 7th of the chord will need to be spelled enharmonically). In what key would you normally find that German 6th chord? The chord you spelled could be used as a pivot chord between those two keys. Choose another key and repeat the process.
3. Select a major or minor key. Spell the German 6th chord in that key. Now respell the same chord enharmonically as a dominant 7th chord (only the augmented 6th will need to be spelled enharmonically to form a minor 7th). In what key would you find the dominant 7th chord? The chord you spelled could be used as a pivot chord between those two keys. Repeat the process choosing another key.
4. Form a chart of the results of numbers 2 and 3 above. Do you see a pattern in the keys that can be related through the enharmonic relationship of the German 6th and the dominant 7th?
5. The following is a list of pairs of keys that are quite distant from each other. For each pair find at least three common chords between the keys. Consider diminished 7th chords, German 6th chords, Neapolitans, borrowed chords, and enharmonic spelling of diatonic triads in each key.

a.	G major	A♭ major
b.	E major	B♭ major
c.	D minor	D♭ major
d.	F♯ major	B♭ minor
e.	A minor	F♯ major
f.	F major	C♯ major

Test Yourself 13

Answers are on page 242.

Each of the following short excerpts contains a modulation in which the common chord is spelled enharmonically in one key. The enharmonic chord is marked by an asterisk in each excerpt. (There are two enharmonic chords in example 1. The second chord leads back to the original key.)

1. Determine the two keys involved.

2. Name the chord marked with an asterisk in both keys. (This will require an enharmonic spelling in one key.)

1. Chopin: Nocturne, op. 9, no. 1.

2. Haydn: String Quartet, op. 54, no. 1, Hob. III:58.

3. Schubert: Waltz, op. 9, no. 14, D. 365.

4. Schubert: "Das Fischermädchen" ("The Fishermaiden") from *Schwangesang* (Swan Song), D. 957, no. 10.

5. Chopin: Prelude, op. 28, no. 17.

CHAPTER 14
The Post-Romantic Style

A. Refer to Wolf's "In dem Schatten meiner Locken" from *Spanisches Liederbuch* on page 219. The text of this song is translated as follows:

> In the shadow of my tresses
> My beloved has fallen asleep.
> Shall I wake him?
> Ah no!
>
> With care I comb my curling
> Tresses daily at dawn,
> But in vain is my toil,
> For the winds blow them.
> Tresses' shadows and winds' blowing
> Have lulled my beloved to sleep.
> Shall I wake him?
> Ah no!
>
> I must hear how much he grieves,
> That he pines so long,
> That they give and take from him life—
> These my brown cheeks.
> And he calls me "Little Viper,"
> And yet falls asleep beside me.
> Shall I wake him?
> Ah no!

Have a singer prepare a performance of the song, or listen to a recording.

1. Analyze the chords using macro analysis symbols.
2. Mark all circle progressions in the song.
3. Note all chromatic third relationships between chords.
4. The key signature indicates B-flat major or G minor. Which is it? What other keys are established during the course of the song? Is there a pattern of key relationships?
5. Make a complete harmonic analysis, using Roman numerals when appropriate and chord names in areas that are ambiguous as to key.
6. Trace repeated patterns in the accompaniment throughout the song. Are there repeated melodic patterns in the voice?
7. How is the meaning of the text expressed in the musical setting?
8. Write a short paper summarizing your findings.

B. Compose a short song in the post-romantic style.
1. Select a short poem you particularly like as the basis for your song.
2. Pattern the harmonic vocabulary after Wolf's "In dem Schatten meiner Locken."
3. Be sure to include frequent key changes and include modulations to foreign keys.
4. Perform the composition in class with a voice major singing the vocal line.

C. Following are the concluding measures of a composition for piano by Edward MacDowell.
   1. Have a member of the class who is a piano major play the excerpt.
   2. Using letter symbols and slurs, make a complete macro analysis of the chords and progressions.
   3. Based on the chords identified in your macro analysis, make a complete Roman numeral analysis of the excerpt.
   4. Circle all nonharmonic tones on the score and label them by type name.
   5. Discuss the chromatic chords, as well as the nonharmonic tones, and their treatment.
   6. Determine if tonal instability and nonfunctional harmony are evident in the excerpt.
   7. Write a short paper summarizing your findings.

MacDowell: *Moonshine* from *Four Little Poems for Piano*, op. 32, mm. 32–74.

Review

1. Study the analyzed excerpts presented in Chapter 14 (pages 237–242 of the textbook). Although the symbols appearing beneath the scores are familiar to you by now, the heightened chromaticism and frequent modulations of this style require that you identify tonal centers accurately. Notice how the dominant chord frequently determines the tonal center. Pay careful attention to chord progressions and the resolution of chords. Resolutions are often avoided or delayed in this style and worthy of special attention.

2. Review the chromatic chords you have studied to date. This includes a fairly long list that includes secondary dominant and leading-tone chords, borrowed chords, the Neapolitan 6th, augmented 6ths, altered dominants, chromatic mediants, and the common-tone diminished 7th chords. Practice spelling these chords in a variety of keys. Review their most-common resolutions. Knowing the chord spellings and common resolutions is vital to understanding when enharmonic spellings or unexpected progressions occur.

3. Continue to practice the enharmonic chord spellings presented in Chapter 13. Enharmonic spellings are prevalent in the post-romantic style and integral to understanding harmonic movement.

Test Yourself 14

Answers are on page 243.

Play the excerpt below from Franck's Chorale no. 2 for Organ several times (or listen to a recording) and then answer each of the following questions:

1. Is the scale basis diatonic or chromatic?

2. Do an analysis of this excerpt. Label each chord using macro analysis symbols (the chords are numbered for reference purposes). What is the most common chord quality in this excerpt?

3. List pairs of chords that could be functionally related to each other and give a key and possible Roman numeral for each chord. Do any of these progressions result in the establishment of a tonal center?

4. Are there any progressions in which nonfunctional harmony is organized around a chromatic step progression?

5. Point out three places where accented nonharmonic tones increase the level of dissonance.

Franck: Chorale no. 2 for Organ, mm. 39–46.

CHAPTER 15
Impressionism and Related Styles

A. Using the suggestions in the applications section of this chapter of the textbook (pages 260–271), do an analysis of the second movement of the *Sonatine* by Ravel (refer to page 203).

1. Before preparing the analysis, have a student perform the composition several times in class or listen to a recording until the work is thoroughly familiar.

2. Analyze the chords using macro analysis symbols.

3. Mark all circle progressions with slurs.

4. Study the macro analysis symbols and determine where Roman numerals can be added successfully to your harmonic analysis. Make a Roman numeral analysis of these areas. (Note: Roman numerals can be applied to a majority of the chords in this movement.)

5. Discuss the devices of late nineteenth-century and early twentieth-century writing that occur in the composition:

Whole-tone scale	3rd-relationship chords
Church modes	Parallel chords
Pentatonic scale	Traditional authentic cadences
Melodic doubling in parallel	Linear cadences
7th, 9th, 11th, and 13th chords	3rd-relationship cadences
Chords of omission	Altered dominant or tonic cadences
Chords of addition	Other devices
Quartal chords	

B. Refer to page 162. Make a complete analysis of *Danse sacrée,* which was written in 1904 by Debussy for harp and string orchestra.

1. Use as a model the analysis in the text of *La Cathédrale engloutie* by Debussy.

2. Include in your analysis a listing of any of the following devices of the impressionistic style that occur in the composition:

Whole-tone scale	3rd-relationship chords
Church modes	Parallel chords
Pentatonic scale	Traditional authentic cadences
Melodic doubling in parallel	Linear cadences
7th, 9th, 11th, and 13th chords	3rd-relationship cadences
Chords of omission	Altered dominant or tonic cadences
Chords of addition	Other devices
Quartal chords	

3. Make an analysis of the form of the composition.

4. Before beginning the analysis, listen to a recording of the composition. If a member of the class plays the harp, ask her or him to demonstrate the instrument, explain the use of the pedals, and provide some information about writing for the harp.

C. Use as the theme the tune "America" (or any well-known melody of about the same length) and write a series of five variations.

1. Begin with the theme stated simply with harmonic accompaniment as you usually hear it.
2. Write each of the five variations employing the complete melody in the following manner:
   a. *First Variation:* Put the melody in the Dorian mode and highlight it with a number of planed triads or 7th chords.
   b. *Second Variation:* Place the melody into the framework of a whole-tone scale and accompany it with a short ostinato figure utilizing tones of the same whole-tone scale.
   c. *Third Variation:* Rework the meter of the melody employing changing meters. Maintain an accompaniment that contains a majority of quartal chords.
   d. *Fourth Variation:* Make the melody fit into a pentatonic scale (example: C D E G A) with a harmonic accompaniment emphasizing 3rd-relationship chords.
   e. *Fifth Variation:* Retain the melody in the major mode but change the note values of the tones. Emphasize a rich harmonic background made up of a majority of 9th, 11th, and 13th chords.
3. Write for any instrument or combination of instruments played by class members.
4. Play the composition in class. As a term project, have some class members arrange their compositions for a large ensemble, such as wind ensemble, band, or orchestra. Ask the conductor of the appropriate large ensemble in your school to give the compositions a reading at a rehearsal session.

D. Have a member of the class who is a piano major play the following excerpts. Make a complete harmonic analysis of each excerpt.

1. Debussy: Nocturne in D-flat Major.

2. Debussy: *Fêtes* (Festivals) from *Nocturnes* (arrangement of orchestral work).

3. Ravel: Waltz I from *Valses nobles et sentimentales* (Elegant and lyrical waltzes), mm. 61–80.

Review

1. Study the list of terms at the beginning of Chapter 15 (page 247 of the textbook). Define each of the terms in your own words.

2. Review the authentic form of the church modes (see volume 1, Figures 2.35 and 2.36 on pages 44 and 45 of the textbook). Select a single note. Spell each of the modes beginning on that note. Repeat this process using a different note.

3. Study Figure 15.3 on page 248 of the textbook which shows two common pentatonic scales. Write these two pentatonic scales beginning on several different notes.

4. Spell the whole-tone scale beginning on several notes.

5. Study Figure 15.14, which shows a number of consonant and dissonant quartal chords, all spelled beginning on A. Spell these chords beginning on several other notes.

6. Carefully examine the specimen analysis (Figure 15.30 on page 261 of the textbook) after listening to the work several times. See if you understand each analytical symbol.

7. Review the Suggested Approach to Analysis on page 260 of the textbook. This step-by-step procedure will help you to establish an organized approach to analysis.

Test Yourself 15

Answers are on page 244.

The following are short excerpts from the works of impressionistic composers. Using the following list, identify elements in each excerpt that are characteristic of impressionistic style.

a. Church modes
b. Pentatonic scale
c. Whole-tone scale
d. 9th, 11th, and 13th chords
e. Chords of addition and omission
f. Quartal/quintal chords
g. Linear cadence
h. 3rd-relationship cadence
i. Melodic doubling at various intervals
j. Parallel chords (planing)

1. Debussy: *La Cathédrale engloutie* (The Engulfed Cathedral) from Preludes, Book I, no. 10.

2. Debussy: *Pelléas et Mélisande*, act I, scene 1.

3. Debussy: *Canope* (Canopic Jar) from Preludes, Book II, no. 10.

4. Ravel: *L'Enfant et Les Sortilèges* (The Child and His Fantasies).

5. Debussy: *Fêtes* (Festivals) from *Nocturnes.*

CHAPTER 16
The Early Twentieth Century

A. This section refers to four short compositions or excerpts. For convenience, the following list includes some (but not all) twentieth-century musical devices:

Melodic doubling in parallel	Polytonality
7th, 9th, 11th, and/or 13th chords	Polychords
Chords of omission or addition	Free tonality
Quartal chords	Pandiatonicism
3rd relationship of chord roots	Ostinato
Parallel chords	Polyrhythm
Synthetic scales	Modal scales

1. The tonal relationships found in this Prelude by Shostakovich are quite different from those of the eighteenth and nineteenth centuries, but a harmonic analysis might be the best way to begin.

Shostakovich: Prelude, op. 34, no. 24, mm. 1–16.

2. In the following excerpt from Kabalevsky's *Toccatina*, determine the relationship between the lower-voice melody and the chordal figures above it. What twentieth-century device is most prominent here?

Kabalevsky: *Toccatina*, op. 27, no. 7, mm. 1–13.

3. Refer to Schuman's No. 2 from *Three Score Set* on page 214. At least two twentieth-century devices are obvious in this composition. Other relationships as well should be investigated. Make a list of these.

4. Somewhat more complicated is this excerpt from an early bagatelle by Bartók. More than one approach may be required to explain its patterned relationships.

Bartók: Bagatelle no. 11 from *Fourteen Bagatelles*, op. 6, mm. 1–39.

B. Persichetti's "March" from *Divertimento for Band* is reprinted on page 200 in a simplified score form for purposes of space conservation.

1. Select the twentieth-century musical devices devices found in this composition.

2. List any other musical relationships or devices that cannot be described by any of the preceding terms.

3. Determine the form of the composition, and indicate the unifying factors that hold this work together.

C. The first twelve measures of Stravinsky's *Danse Russe* follow on pages 114–115. Listen to a recording of this excerpt.

1. On a separate sheet of manuscript paper, reduce the full score to one that can be played on one or two pianos.

2. Determine which twentieth-century device is the most evident in the excerpt.

3. List any other devices you can find in this short excerpt.

4. If you find other musical relationships or devices that cannot be described by any of the preceding terms, write them down using your own descriptive terms.

Stravinsky: *Danse Russe* (Russian Dance) from *Petrouchka*, mm. 1–12.

Review

1. Use the list of terms on page 279 of the textbook as a test of your understanding of the materials of early twentieth-century music. Define each term in your own words, and check your definitions with the definitions in the book.
2. Write a number of polychords using major and minor triads at different intervals (use Figures 16.6 and 16.7 on pages 282–283 of the textbook as models). Test each at the piano to compare the levels of dissonance among your polychords.
3. Study the specimen analysis (Figure 16.16) carefully, making certain that you understand each label.

Test Yourself 16

Answers are on page 244.

The following are short excerpts from the works of composers from the early twentieth century. Identify elements in each excerpt that are characteristic of the contemporary period, using the following list:

a. Pandiatonicism
b. Polytonality
c. Dual modality
d. Shifted tonality
e. Free tonality
f. Polychords
g. Quartal/quintal chords
h. Clusters
i. Changing meter
j. Asymmetric meter
k. Nonaccentual rhythms

1. Ives: "Lincoln, the Great Commoner," no. 11 from *114 Songs*.

2. Poulenc: Laudamus Te from *Gloria*.

3. Bartók: Bagatelle no. 1, op. 6.

4. Honegger: Symphony No. 5 "Di tre re"), I.

5. Ives: Second Sonata for Violin and Piano, III.

CHAPTER 17
Pitch-Class Set Theory

A. Following are five sets in scrambled order.

   1. On the staff provided, rearrange the notes in prime form and indicate pitch-class numbers on the blanks below.

   2. After you have determined the prime form of each set, write the inversion on the staff below.

Prime form:

Inversion:

B. Analyze the two following excerpts by labeling the pitch classes as sets (refer to the labeling method used for Bartók's *Chromatic Invention* from *Mikrokosmos*, vol. III, no. 91 on pages 310–311 of the textbook).

   1. Bartók: *Diminished Fifth* from *Mikrokosmos*, vol. IV, no. 101, mm. 1–11.

2.   Scriabin: Etude op. 65, no. 3, mm. 1–6.

C.   Refer to Lutoslawski's *Bucolic no. 2* on page 192. This short work lends itself best to the analytical procedures used on Bartók's *Chromatic Invention* from *Mikrokosmos*, vol. III, no. 91 (Figure 17.13) in Chapter 17 of the textbook. Make a complete analysis of the composition from that viewpoint.

Review

1.   Select four notes at random or choose a motive from a composition you are studying. Find the prime form (or best normal order) for this tetrachord (see Figures 17.9–17.12). Now write the inversion of this set (see Figures 17.5–17.8). Select other groups of three, four, and five notes for similar treatment. Play each set and its inversion to hear the similarity between them.
2.   Study the specimen analysis (Figures 17.13 and 17.21) carefully, making certain that you understand each label.
3.   Define each of the terms at the head of the chapter (page 305 of the textbook) in your own words. Check your definitions with the definitions in the chapter.

Test Yourself 17

Answers are on page 244.

Examine each of the following short melodic fragments and derive a set that includes all the pitch classes present in the melody. Place this set in normal order.

CHAPTER 18
Twelve-Tone Technique

A. Refer to Krenek's Etude from *Eight Piano Pieces*, op. 110, no. 1 (1946), on page 185. Have a pianist play this work or listen to a recording.

   1. Find the row, which is stated in the first three measures of the right hand.
   2. Make a matrix for this row using the instructions in Chapter 18 of the textbook.
   3. Analyze the pitch content of the work by labeling all the row forms and numbering the pitches.
   4. Describe how the row is used in this work. What is the basic texture?
   5. How does the row influence phrasing and form?
   6. Make an arrangement of this work for four woodwind or string instruments. Perform the arrangement in class. Compare your arrangement to the original piano form. Which best expresses the ideas of the piece?

B. Refer to Dallapiccola's *Quartina,* No. 11 from *Quaderno Musicale di Annalibera*, on page 161. Have a pianist play this work or listen to a recording.

   1. Find the prime row.
   2. Make a matrix for this row using the instructions in Chapter 18 of the textbook.
   3. Analyze the pitch content of the work by labeling all the row forms and numbering the pitches.
   4. Describe how the row is used in this work. What is the basic texture?
   5. How does the row influence phrasing and form?

Review

1. Write a twelve-tone row of your own choosing. (Choose notes at random if you prefer.) Create a matrix for this row using the instructions on pages 325–328 of the textbook. Write a melodic line using two forms of the row.
2. Study the specimen analysis (Figure 18.1 on pages 323–324 of the textbook), making certain that you understand each analytical symbol.
3. Define each of the terms at the head of the chapter (page 321 of the textbook) in your own words. Check your definitions with the definitions in the chapter.

Name_____

Test Yourself 18

Answers are on page 245.

The following composition is written in serial technique. Find the row (in the first five measures of the voice) and form a matrix. Do a serial analysis along the lines of the specimen analysis in this chapter (Figure 18.1).

Dallapiccola: *Goethe-Lieder*, no. 2, for Mezzo-Soprano and E-flat Clarinet.

* *La parte del Clar. picc. è scritta in suoni reali.*
(The E-flat Clarinet part is written at sounding pitch.)

Anthology

Bach: Fugue no. 6 in D Minor from *The Well-Tempered Clavier*, Book I, BWV 851. ♩

Bach: Fugue no. 7 in E-flat Major from *The Well-Tempered Clavier*, Book I, BWV 852.

Name_____

130   Anthology

Name_____

Bach: Invention no. 1 in C Major from *Fifteen Two-Part Inventions*, BWV 772. ♪

Bach: Invention no. 13 in A Minor from *Fifteen Two-Part Inventions*, BWV 784. ♫

Barnby: "Sweet and Low." ♫

Larghetto

pp

Sweet and low, sweet and low, Wind of the west - ern sea;_____ Low, low,_____

breathe and blow, Wind of the west - ern sea;_____ O - ver the roll - ing
O - ver_____ the

wa - ters go,   Come from the dy - ing moon___ and blow,   Blow him a - gain to
wa - ters go,   Come_____ from_____ the moon___ and blow,

me,_____   While my lit - tle one, while my pret - ty one sleeps._____

Beethoven: Sonata in C Minor *(Pathétique)*, op. 13, II. ♫

Beethoven: Sonata in G Major, op. 14, no. 2, I. ♩♪

Beethoven: Sonata in G Major, op. 49, no. 2, II.

Chopin: Etude in A Minor, op. 10, no. 2. ♪

Dallapiccola: *Quartina*, No. 11 from *Quaderno Musicale di Annalibera*.

1 min. 20 secondi

Debussy: *Danse sacrée* (Sacred Dance) for Harp and String Orchestra. ♫

Haydn: Sonata in D Major, Hob. XVI:19, III.

Haydn: Sonata in G Major, Hob. XVI:27, I.

Allegro con brio

Krenek: Etude from *Eight Piano Pieces*, op. 110, no. 1 (1946).

Lassus: Benedictus from *Missa pro defunctis*.

Lassus: *Sancti mei* (motet) from *Cantiones Duarum Vocum.*

-tro - - - - rum e - go red - dam____

ves -tro - - - - rum e - go red - dam vo -

_____ vo - - - bis, e - go____ red - dam

- - - - - - - - - bis, e - go red -

__ vo - - - - - - - bis, e - go

dam_____ vo - - - - - bis, e - go, e -

red - dam____ vo - - - - - - - bis.

- go red - dam vo - - - - - - - bis.

Lassus: *Sicut rosa* (Just as a Rose) from *Cantiones Duarum Vocum*.

Anthology   **191**

Lutoslawski: *Bucolic no. 2.* ♫

Mozart: Sonata in G Major, K. 283, I. ♪♩

Name_____

Anthology **199**

Persichetti: "March" from *Divertimento for Band*, 1950.

Ravel: *Sonatine*, II.

reprenez peu a peu le mouvement

a tempo   *sans ralentir*

Anthology

Schubert: "Die Krähe" ("The Crow") from *Winterreise* (Winter Journey), op. 89, no. 15, D. 911.

ist bis heu - te für und für um mein Haupt ge -

flo - gen.

Krä - he, wun - der - li - ches Tier, willst mich nicht ver -

-las - sen? Meinst wohl bald als Beu - te hier

cresc.

mei - nen Leib zu fas - sen?

Nun, es wird nicht weit mehr gehn an dem Wan - der -

Gra - - - - be!

Name_____

Schubert: "Morgengrüss" ("Greeting") from *Die schöne Müllerin* (The Miller's Beautiful Daughter), op. 25, no. 8, D. 795. ♫

Guten Morgen, schöne Müllerin! wo steckst du gleich das
O lass mich nur von ferne stehn, nach dienem lieben
Ihr schlummertrunk'nen Äugelein, ihr thaubetrübten
Nun schüttelt ab der Träume Flor, und hebt euch frisch und

Köpfchen hin, als wär' dir was geschehen? Ver-
Fenster sehn, von ferne, ganz von ferne! Du
Blümelein, was scheuet ihr die Sonne? Hat-
frei empor in Gottes hellen Morgen! Die

driesst dich denn mein Gruss so schwer? ver - stört dich denn mein Blick so shr? So ihr
blon - des Köpf - chen komm her - vor, her - vor aus eu - rem run - den Thor
es die Nacht so gut ge - meint, dass ihr euch schliesst und bückt und weint nach
Ler - che wir - belt in der Luft, und aus dem tie - fen Her - zen ruft die

muss ich wie - der ge - hen, so muss ich wie - der
blau - en Mor - gen - ster - ne, ihr blau - en Mor - gen -
ih - rer stil - len Won - ne, nach ih - rer stil - len
Lie - be Leid und Sor - gen, die Lie - be Leid und

ge - hen, wie - der ge - hen.
ster - ne, ihr Mor - gen - ster - ne!
Won - ne, nach ih - rer Won - ne?
Sor - gen, Leid und Sor - gen.

Schuman: No. 2 from *Three Score Set.* ♫

Schumann: *Davidsbündlerstänze*, op. 6, no. 8.

Name_____

Schumann: Theme with Variations from *Drei Clavier-Sonaten für die Jugend*, op. 118, no. 1.

Wolf: "In dem Schatten meiner Locken" ("In the Shadow of My Curls") from *Spanisches Liederbuch.*

In dem Schat - tenmei - ner Lo - cken schliefmir mein Ge - lieb - ter

ein. Weck' ich ihn nun auf?

Win - de sie zer - sau - sen.

Lo - cken - schat - ten, Win - des - sau - sen

schlä - fer - ten den Lieb - sten ein.

Weck' ich ihn nun auf?___

Ach nein!

Hö - ren muss ich, wie ihn grä - me, dass er schmach - tet schon so

lan - ge, dass ihm Le - ben geb' und neh - me die - se mei - ne brau - ne Wan - - - - ge.

Und er nennt mich sei - ne Schlan - ge,

sehr zurückhaltend

und doch schlief er bei__ mir ein.

Weck' ich ihn nun auf?__

Ach nein!

Answers to Self-Tests

Test Yourself 1

page 4

1–3. Lassus: *Justus cor suum tradet* from *Cantiones Duarum Vocum*, mm. 1–12.

4. To avoid the F–B♮ tritone.
5. There are no deviations.
6. 11
7. Dorian

Test Yourself 2

page 6

2. Measure 1 contains a statement of the <u>motive</u>.

3. The lower part in measure 2 is the <u>motive</u> in imitation. The interval of imitation is a(n) <u>11th (8ve + 4th)</u>. The right-hand part in measure 2 is the <u>countermotive</u>.

4. Measures 4–6 are a good example of a <u>sequence</u>.

5. The second part of the invention begins in measure <u>14</u>. It is in the <u>dominant</u> key (relation to the tonic).

6. In measure 27 in the right hand there is a statement of the <u>motive</u> in the <u>tonic</u> key.

8. Invention number 10 is in <u>three</u> sections.

Bach: Invention no. 10 in G Major from *Fifteen Two-Part Inventions*, BWV 781.

Test Yourself 3

page 11

1. Tonal. Second note (and following notes) are P4 rather than P5 above subject. The strong tonic–dominant opening of the subject is answered by dominant–tonic.

2. Real.

3. Tonal. Second measure (and following) of subject is answered tonally (P5 below rather than P4). The subject modulates to the dominant key.

4. Bach: Fugue in D Minor, BWV 899.

Entry 1:

Countersubject

Subject

Subject (modified)

to g:

Episode 2:

Subject (continued)

Sequence, Segment 1

Seq., Seg. 2

Seq., Seg. 1

Seq., Seg. 2

Countersubject

Sequence, Segment 1

Seq., Seg. 2

Entry 2:

Subject

Subject

Subject (continued)

Countersubject

Subject

to d:

Test Yourself 4

page 22

Eb: ii°⁶   V   F#: ii⌀⁴₃   V   E: iv   V⁴₃   F#: ♭VI   V   B: vii°⁷   I

D: iv⁶   V   F#: vii°⁷   I   Ab: ♭VI   V   C: ii⌀⁶₅   V   C#: ♭VI⁶   V⁶₅

Test Yourself 5

page 32

bb: N⁶   V   f#: N⁶   V   e: N⁶   V

g: N⁶   vii°⁷/V   V   b: N⁶   vii°⁷/V   V   eb: N⁶   vii°⁷/V   V

g: N⁶   i⁶₄   V   b: N⁶   i⁶₄   V   f: N⁶   i⁶₄   V

Test Yourself 6

page 40

b: Gr⁶   i⁶₄   g: Gr⁶   i⁶₄   c:/C: Fr⁶   V   bb:/Bb: It⁶   V   e:/E: Fr⁶   V f#: It^6 V   d: Gr^6 i$^6_4$ F: Gr^6 I$^6_4$ a: Fr^6 V   g#: Gr^6 i$^6_4$

F#:   A:

Test Yourself 7

page 57

Mozart: Variations on "Ah, vous dirai-je, Maman" (Ah, Shall I tell You, Mama), K. 265, mm. 1–8.

Variation technique(s) in Variation I:

Embellished melodic line.

Variation technique(s) in Variation II:
Change of accompaniment texture.

Var. V

Variation technique(s) in Variation V:
Introduction of a unique rhythmic figure.

Var. VII

Variation technique(s) in Variation VII:
Embellished melodic line.
Extending the range of the melody.

Var. VIII
Minore

Variation technique(s) in Variation VIII:
Change of mode.
Embellished melodic line.
Treating a motive from the melody (embellished) in imitation.

Var. XI
Adagio

Variation technique(s) in Variation XI:

Change of tempo.

Embellished melodic line.

Treating a motive from the melody (embellished) in imitation.

Change of accompaniment texture.

Var. XII
Allegro

Variation technique(s) in Variation XII:

Change of meter.

Embellished melodic line.

Change of accompaniment texture.

Test Yourself 8

2. The exposition section is from measure 1 to measure _15_ .
3. The "development" section is from measure _16_ to measure _23_ .
4. The recapitulation section is from measure _24_ to measure _38_ .
5. The first theme is _4_ measures in length.
6. The transition between the first and second themes is _4_ measures in length.
7. The second theme is _7_ measures in length.
8. The "development" is based on the _first_ theme.
9. The second theme is in the tonic key.

Clementi: Sonatina in C Major, op. 36, no. 1, I.

Test Yourself 9
page 66

Clementi: Sonatina in G Major, op. 36, no. 5, III: Rondo.

Formal Outline

Section	Phrase	Measure	Key(s)	Cadence
Refrain 1 (A)	1	1–4	G	Half
	2	5–8	G	Imperfect Authentic
	3	9–12	G	Half
	4	13–16	G	Perfect Authentic
No transition				
Episode 1 (B)	5	17–20	D	Imperfect Authentic
	6	21–24	D	Perfect Authentic
Retransition	7	25–28	to G	Half
Refrain 2 (A)	8	29–32	G	Half
	9	33–36	G	Imperfect Authentic
	10	37–40	G	Half
	11	41–44	G	Perfect Authentic
Codetta	12	45–52	G	Perfect Authentic
	13	53–58	G	Perfect Authentic
No transition				
Episode 2 (C)	14	59–62	e	Half
	15	63–66	to b	Half
	16	67–70	b	Half
	17	71–74	to A	Perfect Authentic
	18	75–84	to D	Perfect Authentic
	19	85–94	D	Perfect Authentic
	20	95–102	D	Perfect Authentic
Codetta	21	103–106	D	Perfect Authentic
Retransition	22	107–113	to G	Half

Da Capo completes the seven-part rondo form: **A B A C A B A**

Test Yourself 10

page 78

The following are some possible answers. In many cases you may have chosen other answers.

B: V⁹/V   Db: V¹³/V   C: V¹¹/ii   Ab: V¹³/V   E: V⁹/IV   A: V¹¹/ii   f#: V⁹/V   C: V¹¹/V   bb: V¹³/III   e: V⁹/VI

E: V⁹/ii   Gb: V¹³/ii   F: V¹¹/vi   c: V¹³/III   D: V⁹/V   D: V¹¹/vi   A: V⁹/iii   D: V¹¹/IV   Gb: V¹³/V   F: V⁹/V

Test Yourself 11

page 84

(Ex.) 1. f   6. c   11. b, e   16. e

2. b, e   7. d, e, f   12. c   17. a

3. d   8. f   13. c, d   18. f

4. c   9. c   14. c, d   19. e, f

5. e   10. a   15. c, d   20. d

Test Yourself 12

page 92

Test Yourself 13

page 99

1. First chord:
   D♭ major: Gr⁶ (It would be spelled: B♭♭, D♭, F♭, G in this key.)
   D major: V⁷ (Correctly spelled in this key.)

   Second chord:
   D major: vii°⁷ (Correctly spelled in this key.)
   D♭ major: vii°⁷/V (It would be spelled: G, B♭, D♭, F♭ in this key.)

2. C major: vii°⁷/V (Correctly spelled in this key.)
   Eb major: vii°⁷/V (It would be spelled: A, C, Eb, Gb in this key.)

3. D major: V⁷ (Correctly spelled in this key.)
   Db major: Gr⁶ (It would be spelled: Bbb, Db, Fb, G in this key.)

4. Ab major: vii°⁷ (It would be spelled: G, Bb, Db, Fb in this key.)
   Cb major: vii°⁷ (Correctly spelled in this key.)

5. Ab major: Gr⁶ (It would be spelled: Fb, Ab, Cb, E in this key.)
   A major: V⁷ (Correctly spelled in this key.)

Test Yourself 14
page 104

1. The excerpt is quite chromatic, but there is some evidence of functional harmony (note the circle progressions).

2. The most common chord quality is the Mm7th chord (dominant 7th).

Franck: Chorale no. 2 for Organ, mm. 39–46.

3. Chords 5–6 could be: E: ii V⁷.
   Chords 7–8 could be: D: Gr⁶ V⁷.
   Chords 8–9 could be: D: V⁷ I.
   Chords 7–9 create a strong cadence in D major: Gr⁶ V⁷ I.

4. Chords 1–4 are tied together by several chromatic relationships, most notably the chromatic sequence in the soprano: F#, G, G#, A, Bb.

5. On chords 2, 4, 7, and 9 there are accented nonharmonic tones in the soprano.

Test Yourself 15

page 109

Impressionistic style elements:

a.	Church modes	
b.	Pentatonic scale	Excerpt 4 (upper part)
c.	Whole–tone scale	Excerpt 2
d.	9th, 11th, and 13th chords	Excerpt 5
e.	Chords of addition and omission	
f.	Quartal/quintal chords	Excerpt 1
g.	Linear cadence	
h.	Third–relationship cadence	Excerpt 3 (enharmonic)
i.	Melodic doubling at various intervals	Excerpt 4
j.	Parallel chords (planing)	Excerpts 1, 3

Test Yourself 16

page 116

a.	Pandiatonicism	Excerpt 2
b.	Polytonality	Excerpts 3, 5
c.	Dual modality	
d.	Shifted tonality	
e.	Free tonality	
f.	Polychords	Excerpts 1, 2, 4, 5
g.	Quartal/quintal chords	Excerpt 5
h.	Clusters	Excerpt 1
i.	Changing meter	Excerpt 5
j.	Asymmetric meter	
k.	Nonaccentual rhythms	Excerpt 1

Test Yourself 17

page 120

Test Yourself 18

page 122

Dallapiccola: *Goethe-Lieder*, no. 2, for Mezzo-Soprano and E-flat Clarinet.

	I^0	I^1	I^{11}	I^9	I^3	I^8	I^6	I^7	I^2	I^5	I^4	I^{10}	
P^0	G♯	A	G	F	B	E	D	D♯	A♯	C♯	C	F♯	R^0
P^{11}	G	G♯	F♯	E	A♯	D♯	C♯	D	A	C	B	F	R^{11}
P^1	A	A♯	G♯	F♯	C	F	D♯	E	B	D	C♯	G	R^1
P^3	B	C	A♯	G♯	D	G	F	F♯	C♯	E	D♯	A	R^3
P^9	F	F♯	E	D	G♯	C♯	B	C	G	A♯	A	D♯	R^9
P^4	C	C♯	B	A	D♯	G♯	F♯	G	D	F	E	A♯	R^4
P^6	D	D♯	C♯	B	F	A♯	G♯	A	E	G	F♯	C	R^6
P^5	C♯	D	C	A♯	E	A	G	G♯	D♯	F♯	F	B	R^5
P^{10}	F♯	G	F	D♯	A	D	C	C♯	G♯	B	A♯	E	R^{10}
P^7	D♯	E	D	C	F♯	B	A	A♯	F	G♯	G	C♯	R^7
P^8	E	F	D♯	C♯	G	C	A♯	B	F♯	A	G♯	D	R^8
P^2	A♯	B	A	G	C♯	F♯	E	F	C	D♯	D	G♯	R^2
	RI^0	RI^1	RI^{11}	RI^9	RI^3	RI^8	RI^6	RI^7	RI^2	RI^5	RI^4	RI^{10}	

Dallapiccola: *Goethe-Lieder*, no. 2, for Mezzo-Soprano and E-flat Clarinet.

* *La parte del Clar. picc. è scritta in suoni reali.*
(The E-flat Clarinet part is written at sounding pitch.)

Credits

Chapter 10

"Come Sunday" by Duke Ellington. Copyright © 1946 (renewed 1973) Tempo Music. All Rights Reserved.

"Doin' the Crazy Walk" by Harrison Smith, Irving Mills, and Duke Ellington. Copyright © 1930 by Mills Music, Inc. Copyright renewed. All Rights Reserved.

"Lady in Blue" by Duke Ellington and Irving Mills. Copyright © 1940 by Mills Music, Inc. Copyright renewed. All Rights Reserved.

"I Got It Bad (and that ain't good)" by Duke Ellington and Paul Webster. Copyright © 1941 (renewed 1970) Robbins Music Corporation. All rights of Robbins Music Corporation assigned to CBS Catalogue Partnership. All rights controlled and administered by CBS Robbins Catalogue.

"Echos of Harlem" by Duke Ellington. Copyright © 1936 by Mills Music, Inc. Copyright renewed. All Rights Reserved.

Chapter 11

Blue Monk by Thelonious Monk. Copyright © 1962 (renewed 1990) Thelonious Music Corporation. International Copyright Secured. All Rights Reserved.

Chapter 16

Prelude, op. 34, no. 24 by Dmitri Shostakovich. Copyright © CPP/Belwin, Miami, FL.

No. 2 from *Three Score Set* by William Schuman. Copyright ©1942 G. Schirmer, Inc.

Bagatelle no. 11 from *Fourteen Bagatelles*, op. 6, by Béla Bartók. Copyright © 1950 by Boosey and Hawkes, Inc. Copyright Renewed.

"March" from Divertimento for Band by Vincent Persichetti. Copyright © 1951 Oliver Ditson Company.

"Laudamus Te" from Gloria by Francis Poulenc. Copyright © by Editions Salabert, division of G. Schrimer, Inc.

"Lincoln, the Great Commoner," no. 11 of *114 Songs* by Charles Ives. Copyright ©1952 by Peer International Corporation.

Bagatelle no. 1 from *Fourteen Bagatelles*, op. 6, by Béla Bartók, Bagatelle I. Copyright © 1950 Boosey and Hawkes, Inc.

"Di tre re" from *Symphony No. 5* by Arthur Honnegger. Copyright © 1951 by Editions Salabert, division of G. Schirmer, Inc.

Second Sonata for Violin and Piano, 3rd movement by Charles Ives. Copyright © 1951 G. Shirmer, Inc.

Chapter 17

Diminished Fifth from *Mikrokosmos*, vol. IV, no. 101, by Béla Bartók. Copyright ©1940 by Hawkes & Son (London) Ltd. Renewed 1967, Boosey and Hawkes, Inc.

Bucolic no. 2 by Witold Lutoslawski. Copyright Polskie Wydawnictwo Muzyczne, Krakow, Poland.

Chapter 18

Etude from *Eight Piano Pieces*, op. 110, no. 1 by Ernst Krenek. Copyright © 1946 by Mercury Music Corp. Theodore Pressser Co., Sole Representative.

Quartina, No. 11 from *Quaderno Musicale di Annalibera* by Luigi Dallapiccola. Copyright ©1953 by Edizioni Suvini Zerboni S. p. A. Boosey & Hawkes, Inc., agents.

Goethe-Lieder, no. 2, for Mezzo-Soprano and E-flat Clarinet by Luigi Dallapiccola. Copyright Edizioni Syvini Zerboni, Milano.